To Chris
a writing friend.

Light & Love

Deborah Guzzi

THE HURRICANE

"I knew who I was this morning,
but I've changed a few times since then."
— *Lewis Carroll, Alice's Adventures in Wonderland & Through the Looking-Glass*

THE HURRICANE

Deborah Guzzi

CHAPTER 1 – THE RAIN BAND

CHAPTER 2 – THE RAIN SHIELD

CHAPTER 3 – THE EYE WALL

CHAPTER 4 – THE EYE

Dedicated to Cyndi MacMillan
for her much appreciated friendship and continual support.

CHAPTER 1 – THE RAIN BAND

Rain bands are long arching lines of clouds and thunderstorms. They spiral out from the eye wall. Heavy bursts of rain and wind are present in this area. These structures form the outer most fringes of the tropical cyclone structure. The wind within these bands decreases outward from the eye wall. With land falling hurricanes, tornadoes are a common threat. Gaps between the bands are often calm with no wind or rain. As in life, we pass from sunshine to the reign of tears.

Sky Pilot

The sky continues to smolder, ashen, angry,
angling for white, open-eyed,
naiveté of man, abrading
the mental landscape.

The dampening dawn to dusk, dark sameness,
erodes the psyche, evoking,
the melted timepiece of Dali's dream.

Eons escape the smudged firmament
muffled in bland blackness,
hidden in hells of Hieronymus Bosch's,
Temptation of St. Anthony.

The sky, once open, expansive, welcoming;
now leeches life, drowns sound, wars with
warmth and smothers the scents of summer.

The Body and the Blood

Birthed in pain and blood, women
have bled since the dawn of time.

Before Eve,
before the Israelites,
before, and since, the Vatican's conclave
where the contents of the New Testament were gleaned,
where reality was decided by male interpretation
of male writings—
we, women were the source—
          the source of sin, an anathema,
not the source of all knowledge, of life.

We are the source.

Blood is the source of life within
the sea of We, well before the Holy See.
We are left behind as man progresses.
Left behind, as he searches for more fecund deltas,
first in Eden, and ever after—
left behind to starve by those our placentas
and breasts have fed till barren,
corseted by precepts of a phallic culture.
One jealous, womb-less, foodless,
male oriented culture after another
from Adam to Moses to Mohammad to Confucius,
to Luther, and to the Pope.

Left behind as "society" peaks,
remnants, objectified, property born, chattel formed.
Left behind, arch scroungers, at the empty tit of man:
behind the door, the desk, in the kitchen,
the bedroom or the veil.

Women starve so their children can eat,
holding each ember of life, full or lifeless.

Sigils of dawn, we were
born in blood, bathed in injustice
shunted onto the hardest paths.
Hungry, we feed you.
Cold we clothe you.
We, the eternal water
in the well of your existence,
you bleed us to death, Mankind.

The Sowing

Upon the wind sheltered hillside,
the sharp tang of metal and the sting of salt air lay
over a field of blood-red poppies, no Flanders's Field.

At year's fall, fields of rape roll like waves,
in the harshness of winter-sleet, stray boulders bow,
like the backs of mothers, and daughters sowing.
Their nails torn, ragged, bleeding.
They bleed by moon, and son, upon the fields.
No white crosses mark their passing.

For hundreds of years, crops of rape, barley and wheat,
small hands, soft hands, and soft thighs bleed.
They bleed daughters, and sons.
They birth the fields by consent or rape and in the fields
unadorned by silver stars or purple hearts, they writhe.

Today, as May's sun wakes the blood blasted pasture,
each precious drop blooms, a heroine's soul—
acknowledgement, the poppy's yield.

Mary's Shift

Indigenous woman—rarely accompanied by
white sisters—or their men they enter
through a side door of St. Peter's Church.

Here boxed in cool stucco,
and stained-glass, a flock of Mexican
Madonna's shift today to encompass
a fairer sister:

Dios te salve, Maria. Llena eres de gracia: El Señor es contigo.
Bendita tú eres entre todas las mujeres. y bendito es
el fruto de tu vientre, Jesús.

Hail Mary, full of grace, the Lord is with thee.
Blessed art thou among women, and blessed is
the fruit of thy womb, Jesus.

Santa María, Madre de Dios, ruega por nosotros,
pecadores, ahora y en la hora --

drones on—and on—and on

within heavenly heights of gilded frescos—bleeding—
rainbows prism the room in false light, kaleidoscoping upon
the walls—murals of brocade, gold-threaded, catch random rays.

Woman anchor pews with their desires—

Pliant and pleading these mothers beseech Mary to intercede:
for first class citizenship (inside and outside the Church)
for work, for health, for a better life for their children.

Voices of the lamb bleat, dinner for the wolves, they pray.

Bones

bone like trees line streets of Hiroshima
sentinels, scratching the sky
winter clipped memories

Life is Just a Bag of Onions

Courting days are long over now.
Men, well, what does define a man?
Certainly, masculinity is not merely physical.
Does a man let a woman cry?
Does a man make a woman cry?
When did men stop carrying handkerchiefs?

The theater is mostly empty now.
No sedans emptying bushel loads of kids,
no popcorn flying through Saturday afternoon air.
The kids are herded in plopped in front of laptops
too elastically rubber-kneed to walk more
than from bed to chair (I mean the lounge chair)
where they slouch in perpetuity.
A decade or two of total couch potatoes
now glued to IPhones, IPods, Kindle's
not writing, not composing but gaming.
The disconnect's enough to make a mother cry.

Fathers rush down packed highways,
single sardines in smaller and smaller cans,
toward desktop comps.
Carpal tunnel runs rampant.
And, we all cry-on, emptying box,
after box of environmentally correct
reused paper tissues into landfills.

The Spoon and the Bowl

Sons, men, what a quandary—

Expectations run rife,
little emperors squalling.
The weight of the world so placed
upon Lilliputian shoulders,
societally unprepared for sharing,
they're born.

The lure of power presses harshly
upon newborn babes,
first born—torn—unformed ways,
men, sons, what a quandary.

Each soul—whole,
each sexless soul—is whole.

A mere genital patch,
a leaning scale still vacillating,
no master marker of superiority or dominance here,
just soul—stick to hole.

The world has now borne all it can,
it's time to pay the toll.
The time for equality has birthed,
the spoon not the knife
within the bowl.

Memories of Xian, China

O, the heart cries.
It beats and throbs.
Well springs of light lanterns
weave and bob.

Still, dark grime rimed
portals glare, sad, empty-eyed
adults stare.
O, the heart cries.
Its pulse expands.

Forced back,
dark-dwellers disband.
Replaced by children
with crimson cheeks,
lollipops, pigtails, skipping feet.

Small hearts, so precious,
small hands so bold,
reaching out the world to hold.

O, but the heart weeps;
it weeps for joy,
but only for
one girl or boy.

Stoned

In seeming innocence, you lie upon the warm ochre at the edge of a dust-strewn street; a remnant—of larger issues—crushed to just the right size—by killing blows. Before the mob merged; before catcalls raised the hairs on the back of your neck; you had been of a favorite pet, a cherished wife. Now you lie dead, brought down by the bloodlust of your men.

Today, stones are coated rust-red with blood; as the women of Iraq are laid low by husbands, sons, and fathers.

The Upcoming Storm

A decahedron of politic complaints
with intolerance being the first disgrace,
followed in quick succession by hate,
bigotry, and religious reprobates.

The dominion of man, is fifth on this
list an unwise choice you can obviously see.
When has stewardship of the earth been
worse, a politic complaint of no small decree.
Look around; look around at air, land, and sea.

Gendercide in the third world
raises its ugly head for millions of girl children
are killed every year as Man rules,
earth's females fear. Many among the
uneducated live little more than slaves
kept low by powers that be
and greed.

Lastly, the all too obvious lack
of Universal "spine" when
righting injustice of any kind.

Now, this brings our
decahedron of politic complaints
around to the beginning
of the human rat race.

Start where you will,
from any angle of this form,
for each may be first—
first—to stoke the storm.

Gendercide 2014

Gender inequity thought harmless, normal,
causes gendercide in dark alleys less formal.

In India, China, S. Korea, Taiwan, and Pakistan,
girl children when born are killed out of hand.

Still wet from the womb and with no regret,
they are poisoned or starved, seen as a debt.

The cost of their life's enormous dowries;
for in parts of our world, they're property.

Sold if they are lucky to live as chattel
closed in houses less valued than cattle.

Equality denied by fathers, and sons
prostitutes formed by girls on the run.

What of the gender equity crisis, I say?
The twenty-first century is still this way.

Helter-Skelter Spawn of Cain

Some say, the tale's not told
of maidens fair and men, so cold,
of how the dear and sweetest joy
falls victim to the lustful boy—

needs telling.

Some say, the ways of life are harsh
and maidens made to bear the cross,
and lustful boys are not right taught
that they are raised up and not caught—

needs telling.

Some say, the girl child or the boy,
when left unguarded, luscious toy,
are meant as morsels, so deployed
and as sacrificial lambs destroyed—

needs dispelling.

Some blame the lamb, say ploy
though insight would scream, lame decoy,
and insist their innocent act merely coy
so say societies naughty boys—

needs dispelling.

Some say, the rape a rite of passage,
so the multitude of perverts say.
The Universe, seeking balance, says,
The dogs will have their day.

There's No Place Like Home

I came from a land of redneck drinkers, who mounted deer heads on walls without sheetrock. It was a simpler time then. You shot or hooked what you ate. Gas heated the whole house and ran the kitchen stove when wood was scarce. The scent of gas from the open flames on the stove and water heater mixed with everything we ate. I can still smell the butter blackening and hear the purple-red deer meat sizzling in Gram's cast-iron fry pan. The images of that day molded me. I can still see the gash in the imprinted flowers on the homemade butter. The molds beauty martyred to slather the pan, and mine. The butter, in a depression-glass dish, sat atop a white porcelain table with a red edge beneath the window. I knelt on one of the chairs, staring past the potted violets out toward the house next door. My knees knock the edge and the silverware bangs in its hidden draw as I shivered.

I came from a land where, through a picture perfect window, a little girl could see rows of candy colored gladiola's growing, beside the home of the neighbor boys; the boys whose Father liked to flash his private parts to little girls. No, this was not the end of the yellow brick road, but the land of bullies, beer and bullshit pedophiles, far from picture perfect.

Heated Reveries

Mania mounts his visage. Her son's brow furrows.
Cringing she collapses to the sidewalk and
leans against the cold glass of the sky scraper.

Wind's shrill whistle carries away turbulent inflections of anger.
The injustice of life hammers at the crown of his head
preaching to the choir of her, he trembles.
Bent and brazen, relentless in his mania, words spew,
creating a tumult of sorrow upon her waiting ears,
reviving past images of other foolish martyrs and the flames.

She sees him spent now,
the orderly disorder of angst relieved on wind,
and womb into the ear of ever forgiving mothers' love, he sighs.
The sea calls to them through the salt of tears, untwining
his hyper-vigilance, focusing the pip in a caring core.

The harbor view soothes with gull cries,
summer soundings, gentle heated revelries,
love rises like a forgotten lullaby
on the cockles of his heart.

The Golden Hour

Gorgeous boy, your skin shines in the sun's golden hour.
Waves of your jet-black hair, short-cropped like Caesar's
dripping tendrils on a chiseled brow, wisps beside each ear
A bare-chested Apollo cycles in low-slung shorts.

Waves of your jet-black hair, short-cropped like Caesar's,
my ardor imagines eyes a molten sapphire blue.
A bare-chested Apollo cycles in low-slung shorts,
calves taut, thigh muscles pumping, a true stallion.

My ardor imagines eyes a molten sapphire blue.
surely, the night sky is less beautiful than your eyes,
Legs with calves taut, thigh muscles pumping, a stallion,
lovely man-child, whose dreams will you soon make true?

Surely, the night sky is less beautiful than your eyes.
Dripping tendrils on a chiseled brow, wisps beside each ear,
lovely man-child, whose dreams will you soon make true?
Gorgeous boy, your skin shines in the sun's golden hour.

The Agony and the Ecstasy

The air heavy with the scent and weight
of sea green is trapped in the enclosure
of the century old graveyard languishing.
Inside the crumble of stucco walls,
walls which do little to keep
the soot of San Francisco's traffic
from the acid-rain pocked crosses of
of Mission Dolores and its rich benefactors.

The sad spirits of Yelamu Ohlone
Indians haunt: behind, beneath and between,
the spaces which hold unmarked graves.
Sad the day when Christ worshipers came,
with tales of crucifixion and flaming hells.
Came and brought the shame of naked Eve
and Adam, came like God's to judge.

From the bounty of the land, they had lived in harmony,
fed on roots, berries, nuts and small wild life,
their ways teaching of man's place with nature.
Clothed, schooled, worked and worried
were they by emissaries of Rome.
Even today, the Vatican takes credit
for the rising up of the heathen hordes.
Yet, this architectural majesty, art and the artisans
were the Ohlone. They built Mission Dolores, and upon
each unmarked graves white feet still walk.

Lost Child

I see her squirming, poor child, lost child
she chews her nails reviled, lost child.

Her father glowers, his brows protrude
he cracks his knuckles, he's riled, lost child.

Mousy mother, her shoulders rounded rocks.
Through thick glass, I watch beguiled, lost child.

The sergeant lights a match, baby burns
the flame leaps in her eyes, wild, lost child.

The paper's edge is singed, now, she laughs
her parents turn away, the case is filed, lost child.

Through the glass I sigh, she giggles still
another day in hell, she smiles, lost child.

The foster home will know nothing now.
Will the house burn, perhaps, she smiles, lost child.

Claptrap

talk
listen
forgiveness
how many times
sin, repetition
who believes this bunk
this self-righteous whining on
oligarchies thrive on our sin
sins they have created for just this
to contain the life of us, to feed them

The cubbyhole retains darkness, as it should for it contains us, and what they see as our blackened souls. The perforated screen between secludes and excluded as it intrudes on the inner workings of our guilt. Our guilt, the guilt they've orchestrated, and mined, since sperm met egg. These men of the cloth castrated by their own minds, cloaked in black and white, bathed in gray, sit and meat out the justice of God in Hail Mary's?

incense burns
masking the scent of sweat:
petals fall

Maudlin Mary

Modeled   by the skilled and clumsy hands
of artists and artisans into an ideal state of she-ness,
a penniless waif appears   on a stool

last week a stranger called her Mona Lisa.

Statuesque ambered in place,
warmed by lemon-lolly light from
bays of north facing windows, blinded;
she blinks.

Surrounded by a cog-notched
cyclical wheel of nubile artist—
blooming buds of wildness, these vertical sprigs
flail on the breezy bounty of   illumination.

Stick and trowel, thick and thin,
the artists stoke her—semblance,
canvased by millennium brush-biters,
maudlin Mary's returned to the pre-historic stew
by the likes of Claude or is
polished to a pearly perfection
by type A, Hieronymus'.

They are all strangers to her—posers,
every bit as much as she. Royal pretenders
in a world where only the artless

are paid.

Moneylenders rise on her   discarded carapace
beauty sucked dry by the doers and   shakers
who spread like choking bittersweet   through
the suckers light from the bay windows facing north
consuming Mona.

Julie Ford Oliver - *Famous Models*
Ekphrasis

Cornered

The horse stalls seem empty as if all life has been consumed.
One who is alive hides breathless now-deep within the gloom;
and she's waiting, just waiting, for her life to be resumed.

This child had gone missing, taken, her small death presumed,
but here she sits huddled in the corner, still awaiting doom.
The horse stalls seem empty as if all life has been consumed.

Knife in hand, he searches for her; her fear is like perfume,
the blood and sweat, drip from her-all about the cluttered room;
and she's waiting, just waiting, for her life to be resumed.

Outside the stable, saviors shout, the bark of dogs resumes,
she is in the corner midden hiding from the horse's groom.
The stable's stalls seem empty as if all life has been consumed.

The posse finds an empty coffin; no corpse to exhume-
between the boards she sees them shoot, sees his chest abloom
and she's waiting, just waiting, for her life to be resumed.

Her gasps come now like a bellow's breath, rise in heated plumes
as dogs and men come running at the rifle's cracking-boom.
The horse stalls seem empty as if all life has been consumed.
and she's waiting, just waiting, for her life to be resumed.

The Outstretched Palm of Gabriel

regrets rise and fall
chafing at frayed nerve endings of a finite life,
unfolding like origami cranes around the necks of
kamikaze pilots
chewing on bones of our discontent,
leaving holes in the fabric being.

regrets, like and of, unborn children
never growing to fruition, never falling
to bud, to blossom, they decay, never reaching the Guff
pointless misconceptions of a wary heart
first born in joy left to rot in sorrow.

regrets rise and fall
yet, we chose to retain them in the after-image
of retinal flares, ocular migraines inwardly staring
toward Gabriel's outstretched palm
embryos unblessed.

never regret
ever regret
never

The Guff

Sparrows flew to fields where vintners grew
and feasted upon the remnants where they lay.
Each tiny bird sipped wine and then, as one, they flew
off toward a stoned-cold death that very day.

Drunk on life's leaving from the sky they fell
to the guff of heaven, where children's souls dwell.
Small vessels all of wonder, filled human hearts
for no death goes unheeded, each plays its part.

Mid-mourning

The lip of the canyon crumbles
in longing showering lower vegetation
with the grit of rock tears.
Sky mourns for the face of the earth
seeing its own fate; it brings forth
a silent rain from the depth of puffy white.
The wind, full of abandon and lust, weaves tendrils
over the cliff face between crevices of unspent loins.
Sun's fire incessantly burns consuming
all in its wanton wake.

CHAPTER 2 – THE RAIN SHIELD

In a hurricane, a solid or nearly solid area of rain that typically becomes heavier as one approaches the eye is called a RAIN SHIELD. The outer edge is well defined and its distance from the eye varies. The wind keeps increasing as one moves through the rain shield toward the storm's eye.

Sink Holes and Whirlwinds

I sought you out in my innocence
for I believed the press.
You claimed spirit, openness,
vulnerability, but you had none.
Hidden under the guise of good,
you ruled with iron fist
no more welcoming than
than fire to dry stalk.

I reached for you,
long-armed, shivering,
you held a gaggle of minions about you.
Surely, the softness of your voice,
the downcast sway of your eyes
held no threat.

But, does the sinkhole
which opened unnoticed
at the first grain not threaten?
So you are,
all of you,
the wholesome lot.
You rule and preen
disregard and lure.

No you would not want me,
would not want a whirlwind
in the province of a sinkhole,
all your falsity would be scoured,
rubbed raw, the bloodcurdling morass
of your own need
would be exposed.

Cluster, group, circle, sway,
and enfold the sheep,
I am not flock. I am the wolf-wind.
I am brash discernment;
I am the pit of the ripest peach;
you do not deserve my nectar.

May you feast less often
on the underbelly of other's needs.

A Love for All Seasons

Love you, how could I not love you, blood of my blood.
Since you took your first breath,
                    you've struggled and bawled, Christ!
The cross took you from your very first day, damned Geist:
seeking the font of all rational thought, you would
pull wood splinters and lick cuts laced with salt,
search for the Grail unaided; womb or prick; it was denied.

Love you how could I not, blood of my blood. You lied.
You said you loved me, but your actions are at fault.
Wheedling, needling, and hurting because you can.
Do I Love you?

If the twine had not twisted, the DNA not swirled, think not.
Would you love you? But, love you, I do, the kettle and the pot;
mere vessels are we, down from crucifix, well overdue.
Why martyr ourselves on the torturous device of reason?
Irrational love is a love for all seasons.

Temptation

The sky is churning black, black with the bile that you raise
in my throat. I must admit, honesty precludes me
from not noting a tinge of envy—

Monstrous clouds pile high with similarity, sameness,
causing mirrored reflection—anxiety—
            like not being able to face like.
Full—drowning is the air I breathe when in your proximity,
and piteous can be the response.

Bridled is my anger, bridled it shall stay
for what is anger but the path of morbid destruction?
I will not wallow there with you demon mine—

Tears would be a release, but I will not choke on them for you.
Rage would bring the clap of thunder and the burnt metallic-
breathe of lightening the destroyers' tools.

Eyes that melt with joy and love, which seek the sunshine of day,
would be wise to look away from you—temptress mine
Jet and onyx are your hue and pale the skin where death abides.

Rip trees, with claws unkempt, drip the bloody moon in candle light,
but, I will not linger with you demon dear
            in the churning black of night.

Raindrops

Above the sky glowers, maudlin, purple, bruised clouds,
clouds full of discontent, shake and shower raindrops.
Sputtering raindrops descends fitfully, fixed on limbs and lawn.
Each blade of grass cradles outbursts of unruly sky—
mirrored sky, on ocean wave or lake or pond or gaze.
Man's gaze seeks torrents of beauty, rejoicing in each drop,
watching drops caught in spider webs glisten, reflecting—
reflections of larger worlds in the eye of man's universal child.
The larger child of wind and sky rebirths in joyful clouds.

Missing Mother

Bits of me are missing mother,
the bits of me which you placed.
Bits of me are missing Mother *Ah,*
I see you in my face.

Trying to remember Mother's days
of wine and roses—Sinatra songs and beaches,
pipe curls and crinolines, days so far gone, long ago,
replaced by a bitter brew, by tears, by fears,
by little pills, *I remember you.*

I see you in my face, Mother.
Years gone by and still I try,
no easy thing to do, trying to remember,
just a few—memories of happy days with you?

Was it when I learned to read, when you baked your pies?
Ah, Mother, mother's memory—only comes with sighs.

Still, in all, it's true,
    I spend each day missing,
        missing all of you.

Rogue Winds

The air is full of anticipation, wide-eyed,
the woods seems to hold its breath, as the sky glowers.
In wind each leafless limb rattles, overpowered,
the angry autumn storm makes boughs collide.
Down they fall on the tattered cheek lawn outside
battered as the Sabine maids were once disempowered.
Loosed, raped, by brutal blows all are torn, deflowered,
stripped most indecently; the woodland seems to die.

Blue-black bruises rise with hints of deepest green
for the conifers maintain the softer shades
stitched like memories of springtime; they intervene
with the brashness of the blow through the beaten glade.
Though their forms seem shorn, they are between.
Rogue winds pass and spring comes with life conveyed.

Sky Fall

Even blackest nights can glow
fancy filled with harbingers of nascent doom
search the silent sea and watch waves rise
sending skin slick shivers
over me.

Ancient tombs and tomes scream
beware, beware the falling star
beware blue earth,
the temple bells
will ring.

Monks and priests and rabbis
all agree, when sparrows flee, beware
lava's hiss, fissures gape;
the deep plates shift and
crust-crushed mountains rise
and fall.

Beneath the toreii gate the yurei cry,
death's risen, death is falling
from the satin sky.
The guard dogs howl,
the ending drone
beware
the sky.

When Madness Rides on Moonlight

Days pass into weak, loveless nights. The moon blinks.
The stars swirl beneath Van Gogh's brush, as he links.
Comets twist cypresses, a schizophrenic's concussion.
On and on, wind twirls the trees, and does not complain,
nor, does the cosmos cringe waiting reciprocation.
Lightning bugs mimic the stars. Atoms sneer.

Those who spout love, friendship abandon him, sneering.
Their images dance beneath his lids, when he blinks.
Though denied a compass, his soul does not reciprocate.
Through pain, physical and mental, he connects-links-
with life which absorbs and excludes, not complaining.
Nights pass without mistress, Sien. His mind concusses.

His face trembles, torn by the sounds of storm's concussions.
The butcher, baker, candlestick-maker, all of them sneer.
Unmerciful, this God to whom he does not complain.
If lack of mercy is just, may he not know why? Time blinks.
Thinking causes pain. Painting connects him and he links.
He accepts art and the pain, as gifts, no reciprocation.

Voices, the paint, the moon, the voices say reciprocate.
He chases mice. The cheese plate falls with a concussion.
He rubs gnarled hands across his lids. He maintains the link.
How? Why? But, the mice eating his cheese only sneer.
The sunflowers shimmer and wiggle in their vase; he blinks.
Stumbling, he falls trying to sit, the chair does not complain.

He thought God clear as sunlight; yet, the paint complained.
Not God; he could not capture light. He must reciprocate.
After all, he was a mere man, ashes to dust; life blinks.
Ah death, le grand mal, considered- no minor concussion,
He must escape, join the celestial spin, avoid their sneers;
sick, yes, sick to death of not being understood, not linking.

Brushes-he prostitutes himself. Linseed spills, touches linking.
Theo, brother, never would forgive. Others would complain.
Ah, Gauguin, his friend, he would understand and not sneer.
If God was truly loving, he thought; God will not reciprocate.
Mockers do not live in Dante's nine levels of hell's concussions,
they will call him coward. They did not live between the blinks.

Gifted hues, link to sun and moon, lost without reciprocation.
Cries no more to sky, as cerebral pulses bring concussion.
Blood twines. No longer will they sneer Vincent blinks.

The Acid Light of Revelation

digits stray cold upon taunt surfaces
unheated   by the friction of lavender's rise
diffuse sweetness coats the iris of my eyes
life forms in negative longing   to be
lingering limpid a tearful eye upon the cheek
held   in the clenched fist which falls, axed in anger

stray digits weave coarsely, sweat less,
like a basket of ash   ccasting wweave sshadows
upon the prayer mat,   balsam scents the soul
forest born, scratching the inner lining of mouth,
tickling hairs within honeycombed ears,
heated, rubbed raw, rouged   by clap and slap, alive—
in the between, twitching in the curdle of death and rebirth

digits stray rise and fall on delta waves, pulse throbs
of persimmon trail limb ward, trunk bound, crown crested,
human delights all, salted, post dance on work calloused pads
metal touched in the acid light of a limbic revelation

Cling

a brown and curling maple leaf hangs suspended mid-air
in the clearing by the lake, transfixed by the view and kindness
woven within the web, the leaf watches the gentle rainfall

within the transparent lace-like web, death curls inward
its only movement seems a solemn gesture of reverence
with the leafs last bit of I, it sighs, what better place to die

shielded from the gentle rain within the prayerful curl of sable leaf
the spider waits for the Autumn wind to tear them free, to fly—on
with the solitary leaf to see the conifers among the forest's rise

brisk winds rent the leave from loom and upward rise the pair
a spider spinning on the sable leave of maple anchored by a strand
as we our spirits torn, loft, are reborn, within the clutch of heaven

the center holds sound; its claim—nature's umbilicus, man
like the spider's leaf-born flight, we seek on unknown winds to rise
gentle the breeze or harsh the fall's feverous gale, still—we rise

Pickled Madness

Born a wee bit 'early' like a crocus
covered in the snow of March,
an unwelcome stranger am I
to a clueless world, child of the Jew.

A wee bit early for proprieties sake
yet, Mother never admitted such
to her dying breath.

Bit 'early' the Mainiac's
would say *ayah?* like a daffodil
in a soft, wet, ripe spot of humus in the sun,
a budding brightness, but out of place.

Like a crocus croaking beneath the weight
of prejudice a hybrid combine
of drink and mind
covered in the after birth
of woman.

In the snow's furnace Mother was also born,
a child of German extract, a Mayflower heir.
Mother new little of prejudice,
raised at the foot of Mt. Battie
unwelcomed except by she,
was the stranger.

Am I not, the child of 'pickled madness', aye.
To a clueless world, I was born.
Clueless as to the exotic mix, world child,
as so many are now,
child of the Jew.

Comrades in Arms

In the refrigerated coldness of a courtroom sitting with my truest friend near me, boxed in by bureaucracy who cared not for the long, lingering years of marital decline. The unyielding forms of squares and rectangles (benched, tabled and chaired); the end of a lifetime of intercourse. Only one friend had come to my Golgotha, my place of skulls.

a downcast woman
sat before a solemn judge:
the gravel falls

Sedated with mother's little helpers, we sat, she and I attempting, through chemistry and kindness, to bar the pain of memory, no sour wine laced with myrrh for me. The Judge seeing no sense in the dissolution of a union three decades in the baking, washed his hands of us (my husband and I) like Pilate. As the crown of thorns had encircled the pate of HE, so had the bands of marriage encased us, frozen, dead, in the honey colored amber—of we.

Silhouettes on the Stage

Lying still on the class room floor,
brown paper for a bottom sheet.
All the children were gathered round
and my outline was complete.

A cookie cutter girl was I
in bright black patent-leather shoes;
with a gathered skirt, puffy blouse
of blue polka-dotty hues.

Drawn silhouette, a paper doll,
not ashen as deaths cold harrow,
and I regret, my parents get
left Hiroshima's shadows.

Eight years ago, the Rising Sun
was challenged in an earthy sky;
bombs Little Boy and Fat Man fell
two-hundred thousand people died.

The Man of Steel, old Stalin,
passed away in Russia this year;
the hot cold-war was in full bloom
and American children hid in fear.

Beneath our desk we scrambled
as the shrill sirens shrieked away.
The Committee of Five ruled Russia
and Khrushchev was on his way.

Dwight Ike was in the White House
as a veteran, he'd fought hard
the GI bill was now in affect,
bomb-shelters filled our yards.

And little girls with ringlet curls
still made dollies on paper sheets;
while the doll shadows left by WWII's
bombs blackened Japan's streets.

demons ride her bones
while she shrieks till her teeth hurt
pain being pleasure

Foreign Exchanges

Ah, wee ones womb wonders all
emerging milky cloaked and mewling,
each washed and coif covered by linen palls
each one a source of parental musing.
How will they vibrate to the tuning?
Will they bloom, as sheltered roses
or smother at the breast of borning?
Exposed too much,
when is too much exposed?

As babies, they babble; then they crawl,
their plumb pink fingers prodding.
All too soon, they rise up and too soon fall
for the world has dangers hiding.
Those who succeed do so striding!
The bravest and brightest strike a pose
and pray for the light of right tidings.
Exposed too much,
when is too much exposed?

Young men and women so indomitable
who see no end in sight, no leaving—
waste the wisdom of the ages enthralled.
In haste, they discard the aid of parents dreaming.
Risen forms once born disregard the gleaning
and repeat the errors undisclosed.
They birth and raise their own wonders crying.
Exposed too much,
when is too much exposed?

A birth, a rise, forgetful minions bawl
will mankind ever leave the throes
of infancy and remove the caul.
Exposed too much,
when is too much exposed?

Mining Assets

Wales 980 BC, China, Congo, India, Mongolia, Nepal, Niger, Burkina Faso, Ghana, The Ivory Coast, Philippines, Bolivia, Ecuador, Peru, Pakistan, Russia, & Sierra Leone 2015 etc.

Chapped scabbed skin, dirt encrusted, pallid-blue in moonlight;
they wake by star-glow, radiant light; wolves howl midnight.
Insects stir, skin scratch, their tangled hair amass,
almost naked they rise; bore hole calls, days task.

Cracked like seagull's eggs, the cave's opening calls.
The gold-red-green copper metal is worth all.
Child moles, mother moles, dwarfs small, crawl;
between crevasses in the knocker's wall.

Three hand spans wide, a mere two foot tall;
oil burns in clay wells, soot coats each dirty faces,
through rankness they squirm, hands on bone awls;
children, and women mine in these places

for raw metal to make the weapons of man.

In before dawn, baskets full, haul,
out at dusk, no sun at all—
Melt the metal, make a maul
for the warriors, our defense,
hunger gnaws; this makes no sense.

Burning fat fills the air beyond despair—stench,
each vein; contorted the form of those small,
helpless, born, and fills the shunt with continual pain.

From the dawn of time, this drama has played,
millions of children—little more than slaves today.
Women and children sacrificed
so men can get paid.

Schisms and Lapses

Ah the schism, the gap—
the once electrically charged space that now,
seems to hold only hollowness
like a wicker effigy—
before the offerings have been placed,
before the lamb has been brought to slaughter.
The line between sanity and insanity blurs
water on glass.

Laughter has never been recourse
not for me—taunting a perpetual bridegroom,
no release from sleepless nights but tears.
What soothes my "weary wrinkled soul"
nothing but tears.

Hold back the anger the misused fuel of fools.
Waylay the rampant strands of kinder thoughts
feed the seedling of understanding
pity blighted hearts.

There can be no bridegroom for the withered crone
for time has come and wisdom was the choice.
Life the sparkling firmament has reclaimed
for your words—your thoughts
have oft called to me at night.

Lips Part

Yoga breath transforms with bent wire precision;
the salt water satchels, boned and de-boned.
Chakra stamped auras pulse past pressed palms.
Halleluiah meets Om, in ocean sounds

between thumbs
the grass blade reed trills:
a wren answers

bellows pump the bone cage wide
hollow the softness, bowls within bowls
soft-eyed hunter, graze, walk the margins
unfazed, half in half out, attuned

the wooden dowel
sings on the brass bowl's edge:
lips part

corpse pose mimics the end of all, discharged
encapsulated, we of sea, and air and wind
face, embrace, our part, we crumple, prone
still as windless leaves we lie, solidified

Unfettered

Fly
leave life's
unbound web.
Let tatters stream
upon time's wind rise.
Bring sustenance to grow
with wanderers wonder ride.
Upon wind, water, fire or earth
remove the shell, pod, the placenta
rebirth upon the graves of fettered time.

The Gully Washers Whoosh

Grumble-rumble raises hairs on my arms.
Air so crisp it crackles lightening forms.
Whoop—the wind scrambles pell-mell;
the stationary earth shivers before it fells.

Scrubbed clean like a naughty, naughty, child,
twigs and brush scatter. The cat is beguiled.
Cone flower's pink petals lap dance the lawn.
Chittering squirrels hide between rooted forms.

Whhhhhhooooooosh—the gully washer's display,
the sizzling pop of the auto's fine spray.
The gutters are gurgling spitting a flume,
the relief from heat—such a boon.

Mother Nature in all her majesty
has made the day just right for me!

Harbinger

blackest night aglow
icy harbinger of doom
near now, make seas rise
send shivers through ancient tombs
blue earth beware night sky

The eye wall is a ring of tall thunderstorms producing heavy rains and very strong winds. The most destructive section of the storm is in the eye wall.

Dawn of a New Eve

Though raised with poor choices; Virgin, Mother, Whore,
yes, taught the cutting bite, the bloody edge of gray;
I've grown past the mindless role of woman, I abhor,

past the sin strewn path's on which too many stray;
a wick-less, often witless foil, a blunted blade,
yes, taught the cutting bite, the bloody edge of gray.

What role has he, so prick-adorned, waylaid?
He, the Master born; he the Godhead given me,
a wick-less, often witless foil, a blunted blade.

He is not God, and I am not his; I disagree.
I create, give birth, bring hope, have all he lacks,
He, the Master born; he the Godhead given me.

Shield mate, warrior, child-bearer, whose heart impacts
life, grows within my womb and all the ancient mysteries—
I create give birth, bring hope, have all he lacks.

And, I'll not accept this male-ordered hierarchy,
though raised with poor choices; Virgin, Mother, Whore
life grows within my womb and all the ancient mysteries,
I've grown past the mindless role of woman, I abhor.

Shades

Night spills over day like India ink from a well
bleeding into deep crevasses of hill and dell,
running into clear cold streams once shimmering, bright,
painting Prussian blue trees on the high chaparral.

Night edges, the golden hour of autumn days so bright,
merging with the harvest moon, the solstice at midnight,
melting into sleepy hollows, pale in bloodless hues,
cajoling colonies of bats to bank and soar in flight.

Night caresses winsome lover's silhouettes—adieu,
as dark dims weakened toward a shade of baby-blue.
A painter's pallet is the night subdued, as shades of light
bring sovereign signs of a fantasy which ensues.

Eternities Maw

endless searching
mismatched   hang nailed
skin torn off fright
          gnaw
gnaw long and hard   boning the contention
of rightness

wane maiden without Diogenes' light

Raison d'être
not

the tick to his tock
the dickory to your dock

nursed on pointless precipices
role stretched on crosses of martyrdom
nail driven   by a biological clock

maid and man
made
staid

abandon fills the cup
passion petals the beatified hull
dispersal unifies
an Id-less
I

Catatonic

Never really believing
in the illusion of reality
I submerge;
shying away from the surface,
seeking depth, shunning light.

To look skyward is to miss grounding
to fall through apertures
to lose the magnification of the lens.

Swimming in an amniotic flux,
fishing through an eternity   of dreams
I linger,   lolling
in the backwash of hyperspace,
keening to the sound of passing comets.

Surface dwellers float pitiless, pitiful,
suspended in the tension of the moment
frightened and frightening.

Blown bubbles of desire dissolve.
Higher places spread atoms mercilessly thin
denying the existence of matter,
stretched toward   infinity
all life   wallows.

Yeeeeehaaaaaaaaaa!

This thrill? that can kill ...
Ride ...
     Feeeellll the WINDddwinddddddddd
WHIP   whip ~~~~~~~
     your skin.
G forces of sensation
     PRIME prime the PUMP pump for the
s e n s oaaaaaaaaaaaaaaaar y ~~~
deprived

Air gasping open gilled
     life's near   yet LIFE'S DEATH   the razor's edged
path

This thrill?
This thrill can kill ...

Yet, composure,
     s e n sayyyyyyyyyyy tion
          vvvviiiiiibraaaaatiiiiiiioon

Die! Why die! FLYYYYYYY
RIP! ROAR! RIDE! RIDE >>>>>>>>>>>>>>>>>>>>>>>>>>
     the wind on this PRETTY-UGLY Harley's skin.
        This heartless surrogate horse
        without FAILSAFE
        R I D E!

What Dreams are Made of

A simple scene, a nestling seeks the comfort of the night
to lay enthralled, engrossed, in memories of past days,
the nectar drawn from rivulets that run past blackened lash.

A lidded eye roves left, then right, as if it's been betrayed
a corner tick, a slight knee twitch, odd choices now made.
The blanket once a comforter now twists so very tight.

A falling dream, a horrid scream, yet no land's in sight.
Bloodless body, writhe, heave—call out, nobody's home
your casing calls, umbilicus, umbilicus, reel me down

A flying lift of breeze beneath hips, a lofting, oh so, high,
brings soul to ground with sighing sound within the dream
entranced, aroused—the coming light, the end of night, wake.

Communion Wayfarer

A constant consistent tearing
reveals the I in the memory of me.
The brutal rent, the rip, the harvest
of flesh from flesh.

Rouge the ass cheek of an open womb,
drag forth the unknowing,
slap the next ass in the conga line
of flesh from flesh.

An un-whole skim a film of
transparent gore left, left, left
for time and machismo to bore
of flesh from flesh.

Slice the pale sweet skin of desire
rent with teeth, pit with prong
imagine the delicacy as you dine
on flesh from flesh.

Frida Kahlo *Cactus Fruits [1937]*

The Tap Trap

Click tap click tap
on and on ad infinitum
the curser blinks
sunlight falls inadvertently
across my ankle crossed legs
round-shouldered head jutted
the chronic ache
of twenty-first century tech
weighs heavily

Click Tap Click Tap
no going back – or out – or up
eyes downcast
partitioned by walls and windows away
from trees, mere annoyances as they
waggle warning of introversion
sigil sower – sound bitter
the curser blinks

CLICK Tap CLICK Tap
a bi-polar sink hole that swirls
from @home – to in tomes – 2 alone
thoughts shift behind the floaters
in my eyes vertical as I the curser strobes
vitreous humor gels contingencies
the cat curls asleep in the sun
which has left me – unmoved
time weighs heavily

click TAP click TAP

Being Flesh and Bone

Magnetic Resonant Imaging, I aM—Ru—am I,
will the mighty modeled wizard speak, see within.
Inserted prick-like into this blatantly vaginal core
for inspection, resolution and rejection.
Am I but the sum of my parts?
Can the sea of me be picture-parted?

Mmm, it's not a sound said as often as a *hmm*
but then again what do either of them imply?
Does the existence of breath denote being?
The bellows pump, spark, become flame,
flame rises and becomes a blaze, life can be
defined by such small things—

will wonders never cease?

I aMMM, hmmm, you RRR, am I

Mouth music vibrates between fleshy lips,
silent, still—stop

Can it be, do you feel its pull, boxed in you cannot see.
The banging pulse continues lifting hairs
on my uncovered arms—alarming me,
raising the wary volume the hum to *hmmm*.

Thoughts now linger on the lips of What-am- I
brought into being by the aM R I.

I aMMM, hmmm, am I—RRR you?

A damned device cannot answer the essence of being.

Brace the Helix

Circle formed, born.
Drum straddled.

Pound

Black men drive the beat,
jet-eyes, burnt umber flesh,
dark dollies in sari's
scarf's swirl, eyes blur ...
dance the helix
on top of the world.

Single women form spirals of silk
which float the air
only black tips of hair
meet the glare.

Pound, pound

Candle-lit, melon-bright,
upon goat-cream white wall,
glass bangles, bracelets bounce
through evenings all.

Hips sway. Orbs flash.
Wind strokes the chimes.
Dance double helix
dance without time.

Pound, pound, pound,

Jewel colored, gold thread graced,
matrons a twirl, sparkle, how they sparkle
like St. Catherine's Wheel dance the double helix
dance all the world.

The Hands of Fate

Muffled gray like smudged charcoal
     on a crisp white page,
the sky glowered.
With the quiet fullness of an in drawn breath,
     the car sped;
rock music vibrating from the tinted glass;
     lulling me.

Held in the hand of fate,
steadfastly gifted with life,
a watercolor view of a peaceful death;
     the curve crested.
The car drifted.
The fallen leaves were airborne
uncontrolled by me.

A sheen of oil drizzled on the chill blacktop.
Girdled between the bumpers of rusty red rock
within the cat's eye of man's mortality
a vehicle of God;

The car slid.

All gestures of negation
futile eminent destiny was
viewed by me.

The car spun gracefully
across the green lushness of Mother Earth.
Branches soften and shelter me,
wards of Father Sky,
The car stopped.

I sat stunned, prayerful, gifted with life.
Accepted by me.

The Twenty First Century Prick

In braille
bumped out
pinpricked never a curve to swirl

has it got you sensitized
to the scratch
the scratch of skin across a heavy page
word sage bound

listen now to the chime
hark to the voice the gasp
the indrawn ahhhhhhhhhhhh

why waste space, kill a tree, poke a hole
appprrrrrreciate the verve
mind the curve

grab a digital like
hike cumulus cloud of loud

can clicking key be codified to ride
the script of the unseeing
might an A sound *this way*
be, *be this way* that?

hell with   bumped out pages
the scentless phrase
spray vanilla or lily of the valley bold
leave a secret message in scent
a multisensory barrage
of ahHa ah Ha mmmmm
give me a verse
terse   in braille   let it pop

Howl the Moon

So like our two footed selves, they move toward extinction,
ranging far and wide, loving, killing, birthing,
with a familial loyalty to be admired,
paired for life, wise in the ways of nature.

Ranging far and wide, loving, killing, birthing,
the moon's rise pulls song from their throats.
Paired for life, wise in the ways of nature,
the mountains ring with your calls—

The moon's rise pulls song from their throats.
Fear of the unknown labeled in fairy tales,
the mountains ring with your calls.
Your sharp fangs peek from behind a smile.

Fear of the unknown labeled in fairy tales,
your deep, dark, liquid eyes penetrate.
Your sharp pointed fangs peek from behind a smile.
Soon, man will be the only wolf prowling the land.

Your deep, dark, liquid eyes penetrate.
Two million once roamed, two hundred thousand survive.
Soon, man will be the only wolf prowling the land.
Weep, oh weep for the wild wolf, and howl the moon.

Two million once roamed, two hundred thousand survive
with a familial loyalty to be admired.
Weep, oh weep for the wild wolf, and howl the moon.
So like our two footed selves, they move toward extinction.

*Dedicated to my spirit guardians—
long may they roam.

The Unkindness of Ravens

The rye fields' response to the torrent was upheaval.
Hummocks rose like nubile breasts.
Worms wiggle upward toward death.
A murder of crows and a group of ravens
host the sparrows that dine.
Strewn like licorice bites from a bag,
onto ripening spring soil, they blindly writhe.
A clamor of rooks and larks roil.
Poverties diners displayed in a murder of crows.

So must, the courtyard
before London Tower have appeared.
So must, the cobbles before Madame Guillotine
have been sown.

And, so will the mighty fall
to the unkindness of ravens.

Passed Injustice

Of slavery, of the weak, we speak.

What can we do, the kind hearts cry. *What can we do?* they ask.
We can stop forgetting, letting injustice pass.

We can stop buying, stop replying with nonchalance.
Stop comparing our rich lives to those illiterate and lost.
Stop consuming more and more, their slavery's the cost.

Make the market die, dry up, like a staving Mother's milk
insist on gender equity and laws that fill that ilk.

Of ignorance, which so many nations abide, we speak.

If one cannot read, write, or flee,
what choice can there ever be, but, slavery.
If religion says, the word of God decrees,
human property and laws of MAN comply.

What can we do? What can WE do?
Seek justice. I reply.

Self-Centered

Ahhhhhhhh, to be full
        to have no empty place   reside
full of the merely physical
        or of the roaring tide.

Ahhhhhhh, to be full
        of wonder, potential growth   inside
full as sunlight on the moon
        in mystery abide.

Full of man, as women born
        and man encased –
beside.

Bereft of longing—
just FULL
        my own love of I.

Let the Eagle Fly with the Dove

Proud to bursting on the 4th of July
of the sweet sons who let freak flags fly.
Proud for the hero's hearts who stay at home,
working for the civil rights of all, not some.

The right of every human being
to feed his family, now that's freeing!

As the silver batons soar in summer's sky
and the fireworks pinwheel on the 4th of July;
proud of the whole Peace Core and Vista's crew,
conscientious objectors; red, white, blue.

The right of every human being
to have medical care, now that's freeing!

Proud to bursting on the 4th of July
of all the folks who rose independent cries.
the clerics, doctors, the brave nurses
those who prize life above patriotic verses.

The right of every human being
to live life without killing, now that would be freeing.

So, as the smell of gunpowder floats on air,
pray for the gentle hearts who give care;
see through the glitz of the 4th of July
give thanks to those who let conscience rise.

Cha-Ching China

The buildings topple, crumble, and bloom,
abundantly, amorphously;
like Legos' mixed with boxes of Wheat Chex,
tumbling with domino like imperfection.

Clean clothes cha-cha; blouses, bras and skivvies,
on makeshift racks, and tattered lines;
out the gap-toothed, acid-rain etched, windows of tenements;
crowned with jagged shards of broken glass.

Crusted iron, ices peeling stucco rooftops, hovels huddle.
Tottering TV antennas prick the ashen sky.
Megalithic bridge spans dance nightly in purple neon,
serving as a twenty first century tourist distraction.

Cardboard and woven grass shanties hid the minions.
Daylight finds the masses hiding behind white-collars
and Disneyesque props; a devious, polite, populous, a swarm;
coloring the streets like confetti with Gucci and glitz.

Herding westerners with their bottomless purses,
past blizzards of signage, squirming delicacies,
potted plants and blighted trees
toward the cash boxes of China.

Defiance

The tree stood, third finger to the sky,
breasting the pinnacle of earth,
the mound, dominating the passersby --
a bygone reminder of birth.

Wind tossed, branches rake furrows.
The firmament writhes.
Bits of broken branches send mice
to borrow as fallen limbs cry.

Rain-washed, weeping pollen clad tears,
upon the rich and fertile mound.
Taunting the prospect of death in lean years,
ice clad the tree shimmers without sound.

Shelter formed for symbiotic sleepers
though hail may wrack its limbs,
the world tree knows, it is life's keeper,
awaiting only the fire of sun to begin.

The tree stands still, without a sigh
poised proudly, third finger to the sky.

High Bred Reality

Soul progress
    back field in motion
The guff
    Chose, chose, live grow leave! GO!

Leapt from heaven's gold
Jump started into a human mold

    White clapboard poverty with tiger lily blooms,
blueberry rake poverty woolen looms.

Riffs of Emerson, Whitman, Longfellow dawns,
mothers' hazel eyes, father Davidesque form,
chosen to drive twixt a Jew and a screw.
        Magnet of lunacy
Tumbled like an agate into the stream of life
part of the dream lesson
scream   lesson.

Abuser of power, one who had once roared,
 Eve shaped now, weak and mewling
            between weeds of woe.
Care taken by lovers torn.
      Watched over by pedophile uncles.
Befriended by a lewd Father of sons.
Adult child, searching amongst the Word
for the Word is and GOD—there are so many words.
    Root ripped scenes from beauty to horror
Shiksa taunts seep in with the smell of borsch.

A pumpkinseed amongst the pricks of Brooklyn
A wild rose planted in asphalt soil
    Doo-wop   ditty
Jew's bop to a Dago harmony,
bagels, bialys and the French twisted strands
of great grandma's hair.
        Clipped, stripped of family shoved whole
into yet another new mold,
    true believers, ah yes,   fanatics all.
The struggle to survive whole, healthy,
dipped in, dripped in, a bath of acid and Thorazine.
Polish priests pedal platitudes to the sisters of St. Joseph
behind the gilded glory of the church.

Raped by trust and betrayed by lovers,
a rose married to a prickles thorn,
so empathy is gained, and a healer born.
        Metal must be formed in a crucible of fire.
A healer cannot be born without the pyre.

Jesus Nebula

Eyes bulge; lashes flick at the many faces
forming and reforming in pixels,
two-faced from car bumpers to shag rugs.

Bodiless visages with tongue-thrusting faces
form from flashes of light and shadow,
combine to be resemblances of bold beings,
rising to the surface on the scum of has been,
connecting the mental dots to becoming.

Insanity forms images reversed and dispersed
making the straight and narrow a sign of perversity
and under the cover of daydream's sage advice
points toward the omens of adversary.

Faces, legless chase the frenzied mind trying to become,
coalescing in the aimless fluctuations of the *ho hum*.

Dense

My
eyes are
sorely touched
with the harsh flash
of puce and pink-red
exhaust fumes leak lazy
from the line of matchbox cars
clogging humanities sewers
lungs gasp at green, tires lay rubber
like   the wail of infants   taken from tit
dangling arms wave the air   seeking entrance
to the already well come   filled cunts
sighing   rubbing my lids lights strobe
just past the softly seared surfaces
of my   bruised retinas
my feet throb, swollen,
now   depressing
then releasing
the pedal
push.

CHAPTER 4 – THE EYE

The region at the center of a hurricane about which the winds rotate, but which itself is relatively calm. Note: Figuratively, the eye of a hurricane is the quiet center of a dispute or controversy.

The Inside Girl

plinks like the mallet on my xylophone
watch the rainfall, hear the sound
splatter in the puddles

just licking the damp from the window pane
tears fall, there'll be no outside
wet cheeks and runny nose

Breathless

Clouds hang low, muffling maple-covered mountainside.
Fog rises from a saturated earth, weakly wetting a soft breeze.
Mist maintains the connection between earth and eternity.

Within the gloom, where barren treetops scrap the sky, twigs green.
Hope springs with random bits of color to the opened mortal eye.
Soon, soon, a brighter pallet will appear, light will live.

A gray day lies upon the wane and weary eye of morn.
Soon the breeze blossoms wind-born to wipe cinders from pale sol,
melting the chill of fog and mist, warming the home of man.

Cross Pollination

See the gardener's open hand bring seed and soil;
the creases of life, love and endings fill with sweat.
Each of us bloom in the doing of this most holy toil,
see the gardener's open hand.

On dark days when each shadow brings tearful regret,
let shades of green jade and emerald play the foil,
showing hues of blue, in morning glories and violets,
see the gardener's open hand.

Hear the subtle song of the wood-bee working, coil
about your senses as, each to each, some pollen gets
man, the breeze, the sun, the seed, the rain, life roils,
see the gardener's open hand.

Absolution's Font: Mosque of Ibn Tulun, Cairo, Egypt

> *"Peace is not a relationship of nations. It is a condition of mind brought about by a serenity of soul. Peace is not merely the absence of war. It is also a state of mind. Lasting peace can come only to peaceful people."* Jawaharlal Nehru (1889 - 1964)

Await the zenith of the sun,
cross clay courtyard a beckoning
barefoot walked, heartstring undone,
Oh Lord, there's love, no reckoning.

Soundless clarion of tears fall
toward absolution's bright blessing,
within the domed sabil I call--
Oh Lord, there's love, no reckoning.

The fountain's dry, but not my eyes
sounds of grace rebound, amazing,
Amazing Grace, sang such as I
Oh Lord, there's love, no reckoning.

We are but one beneath the sun
for all our fears and wandering
all creation our companion--
Oh Lord, there's love, no reckoning.

Let spirit rise on minaret
and phantom penitents come hieing
all is well, we are God's get
Oh Lord, there's love, no reckoning.

Touching the I

Touching your skin
so cold, flat, hard
the sickness within you
like muddy water after a downpour,
how could I stay. I could, I could not run—
from the death in your hollow eyes,
the limpness of your skeletal fingers.
Don't run. Life seeks life,
succubus to the energy of kindnesses, chi.
Stroking your broad forehead
the horizon of beyond comes clear, clear to me.
Yet fear, is all you feel
and the wind of black holes,
all you hear.

The eye of I, connects
momentarily, bringing roses to your cheeks
hesitantly, lifting the corner of lip
as you, through the we
remember He.
Touching—

Dance Ballerina Dance

Frozen in an ice cube of time,
the oak leaf pirouettes by randy branches,
twirling pixie-like on its stem,
a prima ballerina in butterscotch brown.
Dancing on point in space, it spins.
The scalloped edge of its crinoline
splays outward in a funnel of wind.

Behind the Silvered Glass

Self, behind the glass, seldom seen in shafts of sun,
pondering life's banalities, as from its gifts, you run.

Self, afraid to face the light, the masses, and the throng;
afraid, to breathe, to grow to live, as each day grows too long.

Self, sheltering in night's fears make lies seem, so clear,
darkness hides a mortal's sorrow in a veil of tears.

Yet, rest is night's forte, rest, and unconsciousness;
so, wake my dears enlightenment is the days recess.

Self, behind the mirror's pane, self-reversed in silvered glass,
will only keep you locked inside, and dwelling on the past.

Analyzing micro pores and black grit long left behind
toss the mirror out the door and get yourself outside.

The Softer Rest of Gray

Like the high beam headlights of dawn
the morn is born.
All things are formed by the Light,
and hidden by the Darkness.

The morn is born,
full of dispensation and elucidation,
and hidden by the Darkness
shadows remain within the frame.

Full of dispensation and elucidation,
bringing both clarity and adjudication.
Shadows remain within the frame.
Starkness, and boundaries are dimmed.

God gifted the softer rest of gray.
All things are formed by the Light,
sensory overload to delay;
like the high beam headlights of dawn.

Spark!

Why is it that so many seek
transformation through pain?
Does not beauty, joy, faithfulness,
transform in a gentler vane?

If one seeks to know righteousness,
why foray forth in pain?
Seek softer lessons, giving learned,
make kindness your refrain.

Why tarry on the darker side
live fully in the Light.
Do not let despair take harsh hold,
blind agony with Sight.

Accept as gift this teaching, learn,
don't sojourn in the dark.
Just hold on tight to memory
You light the Holy Spark.

Evolution

Shattered shards of terra cotta earth stratified,
dreams, meridians, dividers,
sharply separating the sigils of time and place;
silently, signaling eons of evolution;
the clay bluff stands.

Soul Flight

Line
Rope
Hedges
Holding in
Restraining borders
Boundaries imprison order
Free me from margins and marginal minds, my soul flies.

The Mother's Loom

Dearest, why cry in vain to the black night,
fight its gentle intent to hold and rest.
Why fear the loss of light thus malcontent,
when ego goes so false upon the loom.

Dearest, what makes you think elation found
from harsh light will frame your hearts delight?
Reality, thus formed, will not slay fright,
when ego goes so false upon the loom.

Dearest husks, of the Universal eye
soft grays will velveteen the fading light.
Walk on courageous in the Mother's night,
accept the silken comfort of the blur.

All that is soft and gentle comes from Her.
Dear Heart, loose yourself upon the loom.

The Crystal Ball

You held me in the palm of your hand.
Handily, you palmed the surface of my shivering soul.
Soullessly, you divined my flaws, plotting, preparing.
Preparedness would have helped but who can prepare for love?
Love in all its hormonal glory rising, raising hopes of the hopeless.
Hope, the dandelion seed in a hot wind of pent-up desire,
desirous of only you, the scent of you, the touch of you,
you who held me trapped reversed in reflection,
reversing right from wrong, within the crystal orb.

Orb of eye, orbiting, endlessly trapped upon the glassine surface,
surfacing only long enough to breathe, fogging the image held.
Held with the controlling hand with its tattered remnants of life,
lifelines committing crosshatched-mutiny upon your thin white skin.
Skinned by your gaze, I retreat deeper into the silvered glass.
Glass over my weary heart, encase it eternally, I cannot run.
Running is not an option for those condemned to love so.
So, round I race within reflection, thought and mind:
mindless, chaste, and chasing a siren dazed.
Dazed within the image of your crystal ball, I lie.
Lie to me and tell me—I'm the apple of your eye.

Petal's Fall

The bloom is on us now
fear does make what's fragile quake
pink and gold upon the bough
petals quiver, fall, and shake.
So thin, the skin, some opaque
blossoms unfurl and lace the ground
each life passes without sound.

Cry for the petal's fall,
yes, mourn the death of these little things;
the pussy-willow which enthralls,
the halo of seeds on wing.
Voiceless, they bloom and fall down;
oh, see fair spring lose its royal crown.

Ever-changing Sky

O ever-changing sky, blue-gray and maudlin,
your mood and unsettled ways, meld with mine.
Clouds seem but blemishes upon horizons
as weary as the soot smudged cheeks of urchins.
Bruised in hues at once fresh with pain and longing,
not yet healed by the riper rise of next day's bloom.

O ever-changing sky, the nascent forest's buds.
Twig-like lashes linger in the purple poignancy of dusk,
and whip Thy brow with thrashing maple limbs.
Eyeless vault of heaven cry for me, release my plight,
erase with Thy wonders, this tattered visage so forlorn.
The sky of night holds so many jewels of delight.

O ever-changing sky, clear to crisper shades of sapphire,
ping with shooting stars, and glowing diadems of light.
Let lavender blue soften my sorrows for I like Merope
need Orion's might to lift my heartache to point the way.
May Thy constant rebirth give hope which melds with mine,
and brings as bright a beauty as Your Venus to the day.

Drawing on Time

Colored leads line the box in various shades and hues,
on my tongue I wet them some—to draw a dream for you.

A scene I'd draw of Grandma's home, white with trim of green,
her garden beds, lettuce heads, and marigolds between.

I'd hold my happiness, sitting on my Grandma's knee.
I'd take her glasses off her eyes, kiss each spot I'd see.

With blue and gray, and crispest white, I curlicue the breeze
and wrap each swirl around the edge of forest behind me.

All my life, I have known the gift of giving my voice,
and so, I share what I have learned, really, I've no choice.

I'd shape my life the number eight for infinity
colored in tones of red and gold—praise divinity.

My few triumphs and disasters were small, and not the norm
more days there were of sunshine than turmoil in the storm.

Though now my days are numbered, I know they've always been;
I've had so much more than many, I've loved and loved again.

Time may pass.
Memories fade.
Feelings constantly change.
People may leave,
but full hearts never regret.

Oh, I feel exuberant, the blossom of my soul,
thankful for the journey, I've seen world's untold.

The Traveler's Prayer

Travelers tempt the hand of fate of time
moving from within one box to the other side.
Sometimes we're scared, we cry sometimes,
yet, to take that step, that risk *Ah, let the heart abide.*

Moving from within one box to the other side
we get a new perspective a learning most sublime.
Yet, to take that step, that risk *Ah, let the heart abide,*
different shapes all askew, beneath a mask of pantomime.

We get a new perspective, a learning most sublime,
a hard fought for understanding from which we can't backslide.
Different shapes all askew, beneath a mask of pantomime,
all are born, grow and die, as into eternity we glide.

A hard fought for understanding, from which we can't backslide,
a call for peace and unity within this woman's lifetime.
All are born, grow and die, as into eternity we glide,
as on we wander, one and all, hand in hand through time.

A call for peace and unity within this woman's lifetime
sometimes we're scared, we cry sometimes,
as on we wander, one and all, hand in hand through time;
travelers tempt the hand of fate in searching different climes—

Homecoming

Crooned, cooing, ahhhh
sweet, soft, she sound, beating round
deep sound, he sound, stroking strong
hunger, yearning, now
pulling, pushing, bright light found
sharp slap screaming, homeward bound.

Untitled

pink petals cover
the silver strands of her hair –
knitting needles click

Acknowledgements:

Poetry Soup: Sky Pilot; *Poetry Soup:* The Body and the Blood; *Poetry Soup: Synchronized Chaos: Poem Hunter:* The Sowing; *Synchronized Chaos:* Mary's Shift; *Three Line Poetry:* bone like trees; *Poetry Soup:* Life is Just a Bowl of Onions; *Poetry Soup:* The Spoon and the Bowl; *Poetry Soup:* Memories of Xian; *Poetry Soup:* Stoned; *Poetry Soup:* The Upcoming Storm; *Poetry Soup:* Dead Snakes (reprint): Gendercide; Poetry Soup: Helter-Skelter Spawn of Cain; Poetry Soup: *Inwood Indiana:* There's No Place Like Home; *Poetry Soup:* Heated Reveries; *Poetry Soup:* The Golden Hour; *Poetry Soup: Synchronized Chaos* (reprint) The Agony and the Ecstasy; *Poetry Soup:* Lost Child; *illumen:* Maudlin Mary; *Poetry Soup:* Clap Trap; *Poetry Soup: The Germ* (reprint): Cornered; *Poetry Soup:* The Outstretched Palm of Gabriel; *Poetry Soup:* The Guff; *Poetry Soup:* Mid-Mourning; *Latchkey Tales:* Poetry Soup (reprint): Sink Holes and Whirlwinds; *Poetry Soup:* Raindrops; *Poetry Soup:* Missing Mother; *Poetry Soup:* Rogue Winds *Poetry Soup:* Sky Fall; Poetry Soup: When Madness Rides on Moonlight; *Poetry Soup:* The Acid Light of Revelation; *Legends – Grey Wolf Publishing:* Poetry Soup (reprint): Cling; *Poetry Soup: Wilderness House Literary Review* (reprint): Pickled Madness; *Poetry Soup:* Silhouettes on the Stage; *Poetry Soup:* demons ride her bones; *Poetry Soup:* Foreign Exchange; *Poetry Soup:* Mining Assets; *Poetry Soup: Contemporary haibun on-line* (reprint): Comrades in Arms; *Poetry Soup:* Schisms and Lapses; *Poetry Soup:* Unfettered; *Poetry Soup:* The Gully Washers Whoosh; *Poetry Soup:* Harbinger; *Poetry Soup:* Dawn of a New Eve; *Poetry Soup:* Shades; Poetry Soup: Eternities Maw; Poetry Soup: Catatonic; *Poetry Soup:* Yeeeeeeehaaaa; Poetry Soup: What Dreams are Made Of; Poetry Soup: Communion Wayfarer; *illumen:* Being Flesh and Bone; *Poetry Soup:* Brace the Helix; *Poetry Soup:* The Hands of Fate; *Clockwise Cat:* Poetry Soup (reprint): The Twenty First Century Prick; *Poetry Soup:* Howl the Moon; *Poetry Soup:* The Unkindness of Ravens; *Poetry Soup:* Past Injustice; *Poetry Soup:* Let the Eagle Fly With the Dove; *Poetry Soup: Cha Asian Literary Review* (reprint); *Poetry Soup:* Defiance; *Poetry Soup: Wilderness House Literary Review (reprint):* High Bred Reality; *Midnight Circus:* Jesus Nebula; *Poetry Soup:* The Inside Girl; *Inclement:* Breathless; *Mused: The BellaOnline Literary Review:* Cross Pollination; **Synchronized Chaos:** Absolution's Font; *Poetry Soup:* Touching the Eye; *Poetry Soup:* Dance Ballerina Dance; *Poetry Soup:* Behind the Silvered Glass; *Poetry Soup:* The Softer Rest of Gray; *Poetry Soup:* Spark; *Poetry Soup:* Soul Flight; *Poetry Soup:* The Mother's Loom; *Poetry Soup:* Petal's Fall; *Poetry Soup:* Ever-changing Sky; *Poetry Soup:* Drawing on Time; *The Poetry Soup:* Traveler's Prayer; *Poetry Soup:* Homecoming; *50 Haiku:* pink petals cover.

Prolific Press Inc.

CPSIA information can be obtained at www.ICGtesting.com
Printed in the USA
BVOW06s2021200915

418679BV00002B/4/P